MEN-AT-ARMS SER[IES]

EDITOR: MARTIN WIND[ROW]

Flags of the Napoleonic Wars (3)

COLOURS, STANDARDS AND GUIDONS OF ANHALT, KLEVE-BERG, BRUNSWICK, DENMARK, FINLAND, HANOVER, HESSE, THE NETHERLANDS, MECKLENBURG, NASSAU, PORTUGAL, REUSS, SPAIN, SWEDEN, SWITZERLAND & WESTPHALIA

Text by
TERENCE WISE

Colour plates by
GUIDO ROSIGNOLI

Line drawings by
WILLIAM WALKER

OSPREY PUBLISHING LONDON

Published in 1981 by
Osprey Publishing Ltd
Member company of the George Philip Group
12–14 Long Acre, London WC2E 9LP
© Copyright 1981 Osprey Publishing Ltd

ISBN 0 85045 410 7

Filmset in Great Britain
Printed in Hong Kong

Introduction

Throughout this book the various parts of the flags are referred to by their correct terms: i.e. the part nearest the pole is known as the hoist, the opposite edge being the fly. A canton is a square or corner of a flag, and always that corner next to the top of the pole. When the pole appears on the left edge of a flag, you are viewing the front or obverse of that flag; when it appears on the right edge you are seeing the rear or reverse of the flag. The pole is known as the stave, the metal 'spearhead' as the finial, and the metal shoe at the bottom end as the ferrule. The cords ending in tassels and tied beneath the finial are simply called cords, and the wide ribbons similarly placed are known as cravats. The main part of a flag is its field and the various designs or devices are placed upon that field. The placing of devices on the field is sometimes described heraldically: the top left and bottom right quarters are then referred to as 1 and 4, the top right and bottom left as 2 and 3.

SOURCES

Andolenko, C. R. *Aigles de Napoléon contre Drapeaux du Tsar*, Paris, 1969

Banderas del Ejército, in *Enciclopedia Universal Illustrada*, Vol. 21: España pp 672–678, Madrid, 1923

Brandhof, M. B. van den. *Vlaggen, vaandels & standaard en van het Rijksmuseum te Amsterdam*, Amsterdam, 1977

Bruckner, A. & B. *Schweizer Fahnenbuch*, St Gallen, 1942

Carmona, A. L. Barbosa. *A Bandeira da Companhia de Guardas-Marinhas*

Castillo, A. C. del. *Las escarapela roja y las banderas y divisas usadas en España*, 1912

Cederström, R. *Svenska Kungliga Hufvudbanér samt Fälttecken*, Stockholm, 1900

Charrié, P. *Le Plumet plates*: D4 Holland; D20 Anhalt-Lippe; D25 Mecklenburg; D29 Nassau; D22, D26, D30, D34 Westphalia; 171 Légion Hanovrienne

Ford, Capt. *War Flags at Chelsea Hospital*, London, 1883

Forde, F. *The Ulster Regiment of the Spanish Army*, in *Au Cosantoir*, Vol. 28, No. 1, pp 27–29, January 1968

Fra Sindbilled til Dannebrog, Copenhagen

Gerard, R. *Heraldry, Conservation and Restoration of Flags*, Pretoria, 1948

Ghisi, E. *Histoire du drapeaux suisse*

Heer und Tradition plates: LXII Nassau; LXVI and LXVII Westphalia

Hollander, O. *Les Drapeaux des demi-brigades d'infanterie de 1794 à 1804*, Paris, 1913

Jakobsson, T. *Svenska fanor och standar*, in *AMV Meddelanden III*, Stockholm

Meinander, K. K. *Finnish Military Flags in the Suomen Museum*, Helsinki, 1912

Navas, el Conde de Las. *Estandarte Real*

Niox, G. L. *Drapeaux et Trophées*, Paris, 1910

Over, K. *Flags & Standards of the Napoleonic Wars*, London, 1976

Pivka, Otto von. *The Black Brunswickers*, London 1973

Pivka, Otto von. *Dutch-Belgian Troops of the Napoleonic Wars*, London, 1980

Pivka, Otto von. *Napoleon's German Allies 1: Westphalia & Kleve-Berg*, London, 1975

(All Men-at-Arms series.)

Sales, E. A. Pereira de. *Bandeiras e Estandartes . . .*, Lisbon, 1930

Schirmer, F. *Das Celler Soldatenbuch . . .*, 1937

Servicio Historico Militar. *Heraldica e Historiales del Ejercito*, Vols 1 & 2, Madrid, 1969; Vol 3, Madrid 1973

Soto, S. M. de. (Conde de Clonard). *Album de la Caballeria Espagnol*, 1861

Soto, S. M. de. (Conde de Clonard). *Historia orgãnica de la Infanteria y la Caballeria*, 1856

Wappen und Flaggen des Deutschen Reiches und seiner Bundesstaaten, Dortmund, 1979

The author also wishes to acknowledge the considerable assistance so generously given by the following institutions and individuals over the years: Arquivo Historico Militar, Lisbon; Biblioteca Nacional de Lisboa; Gunvor Klingberg, curator of the Kungl. Armeemuseum, Stockholm; Mr Green, librarian to the Luso-British Council's library, London; Musée de l'Armée, Paris; Christina Cleeve, assistant curator at the Museovirasto, Helsinki, and Professor Ole Gripenberg, also of Helsinki; Servicio Histórico Militar, Madrid; Ignacio de Ribot y de Balle; Tony Burgess; Joaquin Pla Dalmau; Alan Hansford Waters; Richard Howard; Peter Hofschröer; Furio Lorenzetti; Louis Mühlemann; Captain H. Ringoir; and Kl. Sierksma.

Anhalt-Lippe

In 1806 the lesser German states were persuaded to form the Confederation of the Rhine, and contingents from these states were banded together to form Rheinbund regiments. The 5th Rheinbund-Regiment consisted of two battalions,

1. Waldeck-Lippe and Schaumburg-Lippe Landwehr battalions, 1814–15 (reverse). Note that fuller descriptions of flags illustrated here in black and white are given in the text under the appropriate national headings.

the 1st from Anhalt, the 2nd from Lippe.

The flag of the 1st Battalion was presented in May 1807 and measured 80 by 70cm. It was white, and in the centre of the obverse bore an escutcheon of the arms of Anhalt and Saxony: see Plate A2 for detail, the only difference being that the white ribbon bearing the word ANHALT was missing from the 1807 model. The reverse bore in the centre just the one word, ANHALT. The gilt finial for this flag had formerly belonged to the old Chasseurs de Dessau regiment (incorporated in the 1st Battalion) and is also illustrated in Plate A2. The stave was white. This flag was destroyed in Spain at the combat of La Bisbal on 4 September 1810, though the stave, finial, cords and a fragment of the flag were saved by the colour sergeant.

A new flag was issued on 14 May 1811, on the same white stave with the old Chasseur finial, and of the same pattern as the obverse of the 1807 model, except a white ribbon bearing the word ANHALT was now draped across the arms: see Plate A2. Both sides of the flag now bore the same design. The battalion capitulated at Danzig in 1813, but was allowed to retain its flag.

The 2nd Battalion of the 5th Rheinbund-Regiment did not receive a flag until 23 August 1812, when it was presented with the flag illustrated in Plate A1 (reverse): the size was 105cm on the stave by 100cm in the fly. The obverse was of the same basic design but bore in gold in the central diamond the words MUTH/UND/AUSDAUER, while the four coats of arms were also different: 1, red rose on white field (Lippe); 2, red star on yellow field (Sternberg); 3, the arms of Anhalt; 4, black bear on white over blue field (Bernberg). This flag was carried on the Russian campaign and survived to be returned to Lippe.

The stave for the 2nd Battalion's flag was also white, 265cm long, surmounted by a spearhead-shaped finial 23cm high bearing the monogram FL (Fürsten Leopold), and with a 9cm-long ferrule. Both ferrule and finial were gilt.

New regiments were raised at the end of 1813 when the German states defected to the Allies, and these took part in the 1814 campaign against the French. The Waldeck-Lippe and Schaumburg-Lippe Landwehr unit carried the flag illustrated in Fig 1: green field, all decoration in gold. The obverse was of the same design but bore in the centre of the wreath a crown, with below it three shields, left to right: 1, red rose on white field (Lippe); 2, black eight-pointed star on yellow field (Waldeck); 3, white field with red indented border, and in the centre an escutcheon divided white over red (Holstein).

The regular battalions may have used this same pattern, possibly on a white field, and with bundles of arrows in place of the crosses.

Berg

In early 1806 Napoleon united Berg and Kleve (together with parts of Munster and Nassau) and gave control to Joachim Murat. Murat designed flags for the tiny force of his duchy and these seem to have been presented to the 1st Berg Infantry Regiment (four battalions) and the Chevau-légers regiment sometime in 1807. Fig 2 shows the obverse of this pattern: red field with a white central field, all decoration in gold. The central device was a red mantle, lined ermine, with crown, cords and decoration in gold, the crossed batons light blue with gold eagles and tips, and the shield surrounded by a golden chain with a white cross at base. The shield bore the following arms: left side, white field bearing red lion crowned gold; right side, red field, gold escarbuncle; overall a black anchor and a small light blue shield bearing the Imperial golden eagle. The scroll above this device was white and bore the motto DIEU/LA GLOIRE ET LES/DAMES. The finial was gilt, in the form of a simple spearhead. So far as is known, both sides of the flag were identical.

The Chevau-légers regiment carried a smaller standard of the same pattern, though it is not known what lettering (if any) took the place of the number '1'. The standard seems to have gone to Naples with some of the cavalrymen who accompanied Murat there when he became king of Naples in 1808. The flag of the infantry regiment went with the regiment to Spain in the same year, was deposited at Figueres for safe keeping when the strength of the regiment became too low, and subsequently fell into Spanish hands when that town was captured.

Napoleon decreed the formation of the Grand Duchy of Kleve-Berg on 14 November 1808, with himself as Grand Duke. There were now three infantry regiments (a fourth was raised in 1811) and the cavalry regiment (a second regiment of Chevau-légers was formed in April 1812).

New flags were issued to the infantry at Düsseldorf, but the exact date of issue is unknown (probably sometime in 1809). The pattern of these new flags is illustrated by Fig 3: white field with all decoration in gold. The number in the canton corner was the regimental number, that in the bottom fly corner the battalion number. Both sides bore the same design, and the finial remained a simple spearhead. It is believed all these flags were destroyed or lost at the crossing of the

Beresina in 1812. No flags or standards were issued to the new units raised in 1813.

Brunswick

No information has survived concerning the flags carried by the regiments of the Brunswick Army prior to 1809, nor do we know whether any flags were carried by the Brunswick troops serving with the British Army in the Peninsula from 1810–14, though these latter were light troops and unlikely to have carried any flags. However, we do know that for the 1815 campaign each of the three Line battalions carried two flags, a Herzogsfahne or

2. Duchy of Kleve-Berg units, 1807 pattern (obverse).

Duke's flag, and a Bataillonsfahne. The Avant Garde, light battalions, Leib battalion (originally raised as a light battalion) and the hussar regiment did not carry flags.

The 1st Line Battalion's Herzogsfahne is illustrated in Plate B1 and B2, its Bataillonsfahne in Fig 4: yellow fields with light blue lozenge, silver fringe, corner emblems, horse and lettering. The ducal arms on the reverse are as shown in Plate B2. Both flags were approximately 140cm square, carried on a stave three metres long with a gilt finial bearing the duke's monogram above the horse of Hanover.

The 2nd Line Battalion's Herzogsfahne is illustrated in Plate B3 and B4, and its Bataillons-fahne in Fig 5: light blue field with black band as shown, the ducal arms in proper colours, all other decoration in silver. The flags were 140cm square.

The 3rd Battalion's Herzogsfahne was light blue with all decoration in silver: in the centre the horse of Hanover with above it a crown, and above that the motto NUNQUAM RETRORSUM. In each corner was a crown above the duke's monogram. Both sides bore the same design and the flag measured 144 by 150cm. The Bataillonsfahne was 142cm square and had a broad black border, leaving a central square which was light blue on the reverse, yellow on the obverse. The centre of the reverse bore a horse with the motto NUNQUAM RETRORSUM above it, all in silver. The obverse had a wreath topped by a crown, and a motto within the wreath reading MIT GOTT/FÜR FÜRST/UND/VATERLAND/MDCCCXIV. Below the knot tying the wreath was a small death's-head. All this decoration was again in silver. Both flags had golden cravats and light blue cords. The finial was circular, topped by the

3. Grand Duchy of Kleve-Berg units, 1809 pattern (obverse).

4. Brunswick: Bataillonsfahne, 1st Line Battalion, 1815.

5. Brunswick: Bataillonsfahne, 2nd Line Battalion, 1815.

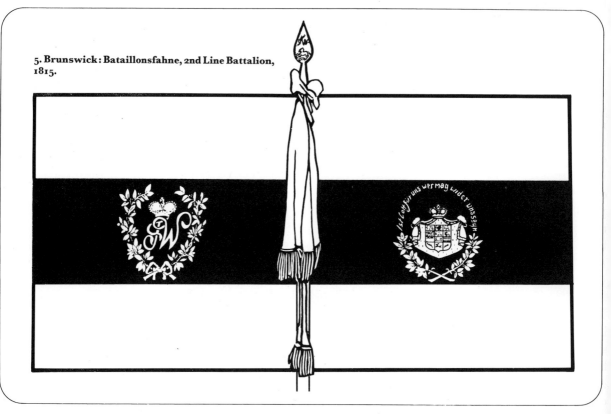

ducal crown, the circular part bearing the duke's monogram above the date '1814'.

Denmark

On 31 October 1807 the dual kingdom of Denmark and Norway allied itself with France, and at the beginning of November declared war on Britain. At this date, and for the remainder of the Napoleonic Wars, the regiments of the kingdom carried flags of the patterns issued in or around 1780.

For infantry regiments there were two distinct patterns: a national flag, illustrated by Fig 6 (red field with white cross, green wreaths and gold cyphers); and a regimental flag, illustrated by Fig 7; gold shield, crown and cyphers, green wreaths, red hearts and blue lion on the shield, a canton of the Dannebrog or national flag, white 'flames', and field in various colours according to regiment —in this case a black field. (The central shield in the illustration is probably incorrect: it is more likely to have been without the top 'corners', the shield being angled in towards the crown instead.)

Over (see Sources list) states that a regiment's grenadier company (in the 1st Battalion) carried the national flag, and the 3rd and 4th Battalions of a regiment each carried two national flags, while the 1st and 2nd Battalions each carried two regimental flags. This seems a rather strange arrangement (in most countries the norm was for each battalion to carry one national and one regimental flag), but I have been unable to either confirm or refute the statement. Size was about 132cm square. Field colours for other infantry regiments in 1812–13 were: Queen's Regt., light blue; Oldenburg Regt., green (given as black for 1809); Holstein Regt., green; Fyeri Regt., white; Jutland Regt., black.

The Royal Horse Guards (Den Kongelige Livgarde Til Hast) bore standards of the design illustrated in Plate A3; that of the 1st or Liveskadronen is shown. The 2nd Squadron's standard had a red field. No other details are known of the 2nd Squadron's standard, but it is most likely the design was as for the 1st Squadron.

The Light Dragoon regiments carried one standard for each squadron (establishment was four squadrons), each measuring 55 by 64cm and carried on a stave 250cm long. All were of the same pattern, illustrated in Plate A4, with the field in the regiment's facing colour—only that of the Holstein and Jutland Light Dragoon Regiment in 1813 is known. The heavy cavalry regiment Holstenke Ryttere had grass green facings in 1813. No details are known of its standards, but they might have been of the same design as those of the Light Dragoons.

The Jutland Hussar Regiment had two standards, one for each squadron, measuring approximately 55 by 64cm. The field was crimson (the regiment's facing colour) and bore on one side the king's monogram in silver and on the other a silver dove with a blue ribbon in its beak.

Finland

Finland was invaded by Russia on 8 February 1808, an invasion resisted by the army of the dual kingdom of Sweden and Finland. In September 1809 Finland was ceded to Russia by Sweden, and became a self-governing Grand Duchy under the Tsar. During the period 1792–1809 the Finnish regiments of the dual kingdom carried flags of the pattern approved in 1766.

Each infantry regiment had eight flags, a Liffana or Life flag with a white field, carried by the Life Company, and seven coloured Kompanifana carried by the other seven companies of the regiment. A central device, illustrated in Figs 8 and 9, was common to all these colours, but the arms within that device differed, being the arms of the various provinces within which the regiments were raised, and after which they were named. Fig 8 shows a Kompanifana of the Åbo (Turku in Finnish) Infantry Regiment, a dark red field with all-gold decoration; and Fig 9 a Kompanifana of the Nylands (Uusimaa in Finnish) Infantry Regiment, red field, all-gold central emblem except for yellow flags bearing blue crosses.

Light infantry and artillery units did not carry flags. Volunteer corps, militia and enlisted regiments carried flags of designs chosen by their commanders, which led to a great variety of designs. (There were two types of regiment, those raised under a military tenure system, i.e. the provincial regiments, and the enlisted regiments, which included all artillery and light infantry units, as well as some infantry and cavalry regiments.)

The Finnish Guard Regiment carried the flag illustrated by Fig 10. This flag survives in Leningrad, but I have been unable to discover the colours of the field.

All these flags were carried on staves with a gilt finial in the form of a pierced spearhead, bearing the royal monogram with a crown above it.

Cavalry and dragoon regiments had one standard or swallow-tailed guidon per squadron. The standard measured approximately 65cm square, the guidon 108cm overall by 92cm on the hoist. The obverse bore the sovereign's monogram within palm leaves and with a crown overall, the reverse a provincial coat of arms. Liffana were white, Kompanifana coloured. Figs 11 and 12 illustrate the pattern: the reverse and obverse of the guidon carried by the Nylands Dragoon Regiment, field red, fringe and decoration gold except parts of the helmet and the flags on the reverse are yellow, the crosses on the flags blue. The size of this particular example is 70cm on the hoist, 58cm to the fork, 93cm overall in the fly.

The guidon carried by the Livdragonregementet in 1814–15 is illustrated by Fig 13: white field with all-gold embroidery, except the arms of Finland are in their proper colours. Size is 71cm on the hoist, 61cm to the fork, and 82cm overall in the fly.

Hanover

The electorate of Hanover was occupied by Prussia in 1801 and 1805, and by France in 1803 and 1806: on the last occasion Napoleon incorporated the southern part of the electorate in the new kingdom of Westphalia, adding the northern part to France in 1810.

As a result of these occupations, part of the former army of the electorate served in the French Army, as the Légion Hanovrienne, but a much larger number of Hanoverians preferred to serve with the British Army from 1803 onwards, and as the King's German Legion served with distinction in the Peninsula and in the Waterloo campaign. The flags of the King's German Legion have been dealt with in *Flags of the Napoleonic Wars (2)*, Men-at-Arms 78.

The Légion Hanovrienne was formed on 12 August 1803 and consisted of one battalion of light infantry and a regiment of Chasseurs à cheval of four squadrons: a second light infantry battalion was formed on 10 March 1810 from Westphalians. Due to heavy losses in the Peninsula, the legion was disbanded on 11 August 1811, the survivors going to the 3rd and 4th Foreign Regiments, and 127th, 128th and 129th Line.

In December 1804 the Minister of War ordered the manufacture and presentation to the legion of flags of the French 1804 pattern, to be carried on a blue stave with a plain gilt finial of spearhead-shape instead of the French eagle. The pattern is illustrated in Plate C1 and C2.

Hanover was freed from French domination in 1813 and was able to reform her own army. The rather archaic pre-1803 flags were not reintroduced, and in 1813 the few known flags, at least, did not follow any basic pattern, but were rather expressions of patriotic feelings by individuals. Fig 14 shows the flag carried by Kielmansegge's Jäger Corps in 1813; Fig 15 that of the Feldbataillon Hoya, black field, white decoration. The stave of the latter was blue. The Feldbataillon Calenburg had a 126 by 128cm white flag with a central wreath of laurel (left) and oak (right) leaves, inside which on one side was the inscription ZIEHT AUS/ZUM EDLEN/KAMPF and on the other KEHRT/HEIM MIT/SIEG/GEKROENET. Just below the knot on the wreath was the date 'AO 1813'. The flag was fringed.

The Landwehr Bataillon Gifhorn carried in 1815 a yellow flag measuring 100 by 180cm, again fringed. The central design was an oak tree, in front of which was a silver horse of Hanover facing the fly and with a crown above it. Below this was an inscription, the last word of which was GIFHORN: the rest of the inscription is not known, but may simply have been LANDWEHR BATAILLON

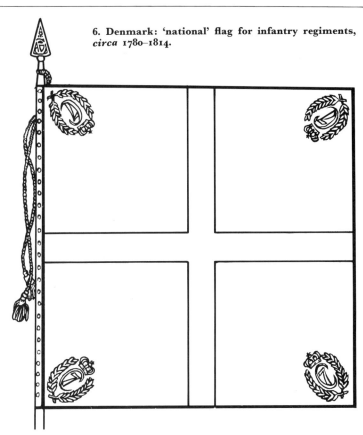

6. Denmark: 'national' flag for infantry regiments, *circa* 1780–1814.

7. Denmark: 'regimental' flag for infantry regiments, *circa* 1780–1814.

GIFHORN. The flag was carried on a blue stave and had yellow cords. No other details are known of the flags carried in 1815.

A fringed flag carried by an unidentified infantry regiment in 1813 is illustrated in Over's book: white field bearing on the obverse the white horse of Hanover on a red disc, around which is the inscription QUO FAS ET GLORIA DUCUNT, and on the reverse a white disc bearing a crowned 'GR III' cypher, within a red embroidered border.

Hesse

Louis X, Landgrave of Hesse, joined the French cause in 1806 and with the formation of the Rheinbund gained new lands and was able to assume the title of Grand Duke Louis I of Hesse. He contributed three infantry regiments, each of two battalions, to the Confederation, together with three cavalry regiments and an artillery contingent.

The infantry regiments carried two flags per battalion, each flag measuring 130cm square and carried on a stave 315cm long. The basic design for these flags, used from 1804 until the end of 1813, was as shown in Fig 16, the Leibfahne of the Leib Regiment. (The drawing shows the flag as it appeared before 1804: in the 1804 pattern the colour or colours of the corner 'rays' appeared behind the corner wreaths and cyphers.) This particular flag had a white field, black and red corner rays, a white and red striped lion with gold crown on a light blue background, gold sword hilt, silver blade, and above this a red ribbon bearing a motto in gold. All wreaths were green with red berries and were tied with a pink ribbon, except for the central wreath, which had a white ribbon edged red. All cyphers (still shown as 'LXL', that is Ludwig X Landgraf) were gold. All crowns were gold with red lining. The flaming grenades were red and silver.

The Leib Garde Regiment had four Leibfahnen of this design, and all were identical: white field, no corner rays, silver grenades, all other detail as above. The staves were white and had a white cravat decorated with two lines of red and blue.

The Leib Regiment had one Leibfahne, as Fig 16, and three company flags or Ordinärfahnen of the same design and colouring except the fields were black and corner rays red. The staves were brown and had white cravats decorated with two lines of red and blue.

The Erbprinz (Crown Prince) Regiment had a Leibfahne with a white field and black corner rays, all other detail as the Leib Regiment's Leibfahne. The three Ordinärfahnen were black with yellow corner rays, all other detail as Fig 16. The staves were black and had white cravats decorated with two lines of red and yellow.

Of these 12 flags three were lost: an Ordinärfahne of the 2nd Battalion, Leib Regiment at Wagram in 1809; an Ordinärfahne of 1st Battalion, Erbprinz Regiment and the Leibfahne of the 2nd Battalion, Erbprinz Regiment at Badajoz in 1812.

Following the campaign of 1812 the three regiments were reduced to two and during 1813 carried the following flags:

Leib Garde Regt: 1st Bn—Leibfahne.
                    2nd Bn—Ordinärfahne.
Leib Regt: 1st Bn—Leibfahne.
                    2nd Bn—Ordinärfahne of 1st Bn.

10. Finland: obverse of the flag carried by the Finnish Guard Regiment, 1766–1809.

8. Finland: 1766 pattern company flag for the Åbo Infantry Regiment.

9. Finland: 1766 pattern company flag for the Nylands Infantry Regiment.

Hesse went over to the Allies in November 1813 and in 1814 new flags measuring 112cm on the hoist and 109cm in the fly were presented to a re-organized and expanded army. The new flags were of the same basic pattern as before, except the central wreath was now half laurel (hoist) and half oak leaves (fly) and the ribbon above the lion was now black, edged red, and bore in gold the words FÜR GOTT, EHRE VATERLAND. The corner wreaths were now also laurel and oak leaves, while the cypher was a single 'L' below a crown. The staves were now black, with a gilt finial bearing a gold 'L' on a black Iron Cross, and cravats were silver, red and blue mixed. The flags of the regiments were coloured as follows:

Leib Garde Regt: 1st and 2nd Bns.—white.
Garde Fusilier Regt: 1st and 2nd Bns.—white with red corner rays.
Leib Regt: 1st Bn.—white, pink/black corner rays.

11. Finland: reverse of the Nylands Dragonregemente guidon, 1766–1809.

2nd Bn.—black, pink corner rays.

Gross und Erbprinz Regt: 1st Bn.—white, yellow/black corner rays.

2nd Bn.—black, yellow corner rays.

Prinz Emil Regt: 1st Bn.—white, blue/black corner rays.

2nd Bn.—black, blue corner rays.

The Leib-Garde zu Pferde (Garde du Corps or Horse Guards) carried during the 1806–13 period a standard dating from 1770: it is illustrated in Plate C4. The Chevau-légers regiment had no standards. The hussar regiment, disbanded 1806, is unlikely to have carried standards or guidons.

In 1814 at least nine battalions of Landwehr were raised in Hesse-Kassel to fight against the French, and one of these carried the flag illustrated in Plate C3. Nothing is known of the flags carried by the other three battalions.

12. **Finland: obverse of the Nylands Dragonregemente guidon, 1766–1809.**

Holland (The Netherlands)

The Austrian Netherlands (modern Belgium) were overrun by France in 1794 and remained part of France until 1815. The Spanish Netherlands (modern Holland) were also invaded by France in 1794, and the Batavian Republic formed under French protection. This republic lasted until 1806, when it became the kingdom of Holland under Louis Napoleon. The kingdom was absorbed into France on 9 July 1810. The Austrians regained Belgium in 1814, and the Treaty of Paris that year re-united Belgium and Holland to form the United Provinces, whose army fought on the side of the Allies in the 1815 campaign.

The infantry regiments of the Batavian Republic were at first organized on the French system of Demi-Brigades, or Halve-Brigades, each of three battalions. On 11 September 1795 the six Halve-Brigades were presented with Batavian Republic flags, at the scale of one per battalion. These flags were of white silk and had painted on the centre of the obverse, within a large green oak leaf wreath, an arm encased in plate armour in proper colours, issuing from a grey cloud and holding a curved sword with silver blade and gold hilt. Above this central device was the battalion

13. Finland: reverse of the Livdragonregementet's guidon, 1814–15.

number, thus 1^e BATTAILLON, and below it the Halve-Brigade number, 1^e HALVE BRIGADE. Details of the reverse are not known. The staves for these flags were brown, with gilt finials in the shape of a simple spearhead, and there were cords of red, silver and blue mixed. The 7th Halve-Brigade, formed in 1796, received three such flags on 14 March of that year.

There also exist in the Amsterdam collection two battalion flags of a completely different pattern, dated by the catalogue as 14/8/1799–1806. The design of the obverse is illustrated in Fig 17: white field bearing a green wreath, over a red/white/blue saltire, with a red/white/blue panel next to the canton. All lettering was black. The second flag is identical except it bears the battalion number '1' in the canton. These flags are 140cm square (3rd Battalion) and 130 by 150cm (1st Battalion).

Another type of flag (unidentified) is illustrated in Captain Ford's work, *War Flags at Chelsea Hospital*. This flag is of a medium blue colour and bears a golden lion passant in the centre over a trophy of arms and flags (the top two flags being red, the bottom two light blue) and with a red Cap of Liberty above.

The Halve-Brigades began to be disbanded and the individual battalions renumbered sometime in early 1802. As a result, new flags were issued from May of that year, as follows:

28/5/1802—22nd and 23rd Battalions.

9/11/1802—3rd Battalion of 5th Halve-Brigade.

20/12/1802—1st and 3rd Regiments of Waldeck (foreign regiments in the service of the Batavian Republic and bearing the arms of Waldeck on the reverse of their flags—black eight-pointed star on yellow field).

4/6/1804—1802 pattern ordered for all other units.

The 1802 pattern was again white, and bore in the centre a red oval on which was a golden lion rampant with gold crown and a sheaf of golden arrows in its left paw, a silver sword with gold hilt in its right paw. Around the oval was a red border, separated from the oval and the field by two thin lines of gold, bearing in gold the motto CONCORDIA RES PARVAE CRESCUNT. Behind the oval was a fasces with crossed sword and baton behind, and green laurel and oak sprigs. On top of the fasces was a helmet in gold and silver with red, white and

14. Hanover: flag carried by Kielmansegge's Jäger Corps in 1813.

15. Hanover: flag carried by the Feldbataillon Hoya in 1813.

blue plumes, and from it fell a red/white/blue ribbon which continued all round the oval and bore across the bottom part the battalion number. This design can be seen in Fig 18, the 1805 flag of the Foot Guards. The Line Infantry pattern was identical except the field was plain.

In 1805 a battalion of Grenadiers of the Guard of the Council was raised (expanded to a regiment in 1806) and this battalion received two flags of the 1802 pattern, but with the elaborate border as shown in Fig 18. Colour detail was as for Line Infantry, with gold border and black grenades at the corners emitting flames of red and yellow mixed. The other new regiments formed in 1805 did not receive flags.

There is no information available concerning the cavalry standards for the period of the Batavian Republic.

When Louis Napoleon was made King of Holland in 1806 it was decided new flags were necessary. In a decree of 4 July 1806 it was proposed that the field of these new flags be divided horizontally red/white/blue, the central white bar to be twice as broad as the others and to bear in the centre the arms of Holland quartered with the Imperial eagle. This design was not taken up but another, proposed and later rejected (at least for the Line Infantry), did result in a prototype being made for (though perhaps not issued to) the 2nd Line Regiment. This was of the French 1804 pattern with, on the central diamond of the obverse, the inscription LODEWIJK/NAPOLEON/KONING V HOLLAND/BIJ HET 2d REGIMENT/INFANTERIE, and on the reverse the arms of Holland. The regimental number was also carried within the crowned laurel wreath at each corner.

The final design was chosen on 15 December 1806 and flags of this pattern were issued on 19

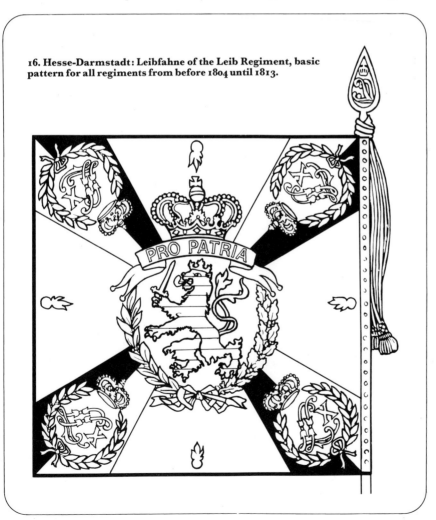

16. **Hesse-Darmstadt: Leibfahne of the Leib Regiment, basic pattern for all regiments from before 1804 until 1813.**

February 1807 by Louis to the Guard, to the 1st and 2nd Battalions of the 5th, 6th and 9th Line Infantry, and to the 2nd Battalions of the 4th and 8th Line Infantry. A second issue was made by Count Dumonceau on 22 March 1807 to the troops stationed in Germany: 1st and 2nd Battalions of the 2nd, 3rd and 7th Line Infantry, 1st Battalions of the 4th and 8th Line Infantry, and 1st Battalions of the 2nd and 3rd Chasseurs.

The pattern is illustrated in Plate D1 and D2. This particular flag was one of two of the 5th Line captured by the British at Veere in Zeeland in 1809 and housed at Chelsea Hospital, where they were sketched (incorrectly, due to poor access and visibility, as well as some damage) by Captain Ford in 1883. The plate is based on the reconstruction in the Le Plumet plate, and another sketch made of the actual flag *circa* 1900 and published in Holland during the First World War.

On 7 May 1808 certain regiments (the 2nd, 3rd, 4th and 5th Line) were issued with cravats to commemorate their part in the Prussian campaign. No information has survived on the appearance of these: the flags of the 5th Line did not have cravats when sketched by Captain Ford.

When Louis relinquished the throne in 1810, and Holland became a part of France, new flags of the French 1804 pattern were issued: to the 125th Line on 2/1/1811; to the 2nd Lancers of the Guard, 3rd Grenadiers of the Guard, 123rd, 124th, 126th Line, 33rd Légère, 11th Hussars, 14th Cuirassiers, and 9th Artillery Regiment on 30/6/1811. These flags were now carried on staves topped by the French eagle.

In May 1812 these flags had to be returned to Paris by post, and new flags of the 1811 (tricolour) pattern were issued in their place. Two of the 1804 pattern flags (belonging to the 123rd and 124th Line) were 'lost' by the Dutch post office, and were not delivered to France until 1840: these two flags are therefore the only surviving Dutch flags of the 1804 pattern, all others having been destroyed in 1814 on the orders of Louis XVIII.

Of the 1811 pattern flags the following were lost:
124th Line: lost in Russia, 18 August 1812 at Polotzk, though the eagle appears to have been saved.
126th Line: lost on 15 November 1812 on the Berezina.

17. Netherlands: obverse of a battalion flag of the Batavian Republic, listed in the catalogue of the Amsterdam collection as carried from 14/8/1799 to 1806.

14th Cuirassiers: lost with eagle on the Berezina, November 1812.

The flags of the 2nd Lancers, 3rd Grenadiers, 33rd Légère, 123rd and 125th Line were burnt in 1814. Nothing is known of the fate of those of the 130th Line, 11th Hussars, and 9th Artillery Regiment.

18. Netherlands: obverse of the flag issued to the Grenadiers of the Guard of the Council in 1805.

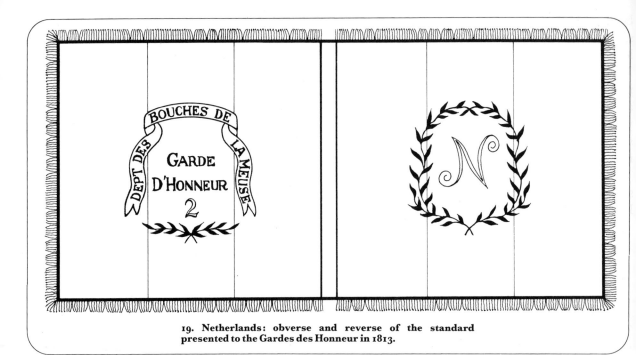

19. Netherlands: obverse and reverse of the standard presented to the Gardes des Honneur in 1813.

The cavalry regiments carried during this period fringed standards of the 1804 pattern, but in light blue and without the corner wreaths, the white central diamond bearing on the obverse the inscription LODEWIJK/NAPOLEON/KONING V HOLLAND/BIJ HET 1ste REGIMENT/HUZAREN (number and type of regiment varying, of course). All

20. United Provinces: flag of a Jäger unit in 1815.

embroidery and the fringes were gold. The reverse had the golden corner wreaths as on the French pattern, each containing the regiment's number. In the central diamond were the royal arms (quartered 1 and 4 the gold lion of Holland, 2 and 3 the golden Imperial eagle, all on a light blue shield), with gold crowned lions as supporters. Above the shield was a crowned helmet with mantle, and below it red and sky blue ribbons, each supporting a medal, and across these a red scroll bearing in black the motto EENDRAGT MAART MAGT.

The flags of the Guard regiments, both cavalry and infantry, were also of this pattern.

Fig 19 illustrates the obverse and reverse of the standard presented to the detachment of the Gardes d'Honneur from the Department des Bouches de la Meuse in 1813. It is in the national colours of blue (hoist), white, red (fly) with fringe and all decoration in gold.

During the 1815 campaign the regiments of the United Provinces appear to have carried rather plain flags bearing a small coat of arms in the centre: the basic design is illustrated in Plate D3. In January 1815 the facings of all regular infantry regiments were changed to white, those of the militia to orange, and those of the jägers to yellow. It is thought the flags of these regiments may have been in the facing colour with the embroidery as shown in Plate D3, though the outer border of leaves was not always present. However, the Royal Dutch Army Museum at Leyden, from where the information on 1815 flags was obtained, also shows a jäger flag as illustrated by Fig 20: 1 and 4 yellow, 2 and 3 dark green, with the border in the same colours but in reverse order, and all lettering in gold with black edging.

The gilt finials used in 1815 were either of plain spearhead-shape or pierced spearhead with the letter 'M'.

Mecklenburg

The Duchy of Mecklenburg-Schwerin joined the Confederation of the Rhine on 24 April 1808 and provided a contingent of two battalions of infantry and an artillery company totalling 1,900 men. The infantry were combined with 400 men from Mecklenburg-Strelitz to form the 7th Rheinbund-Regiment of two battalions.

Each of these battalions was issued with one flag, the 1st Battalion with a white flag of the 1797 pattern, originally issued to the Regiment von Hobe, and the 2nd Battalion with a blue flag of the same pattern, originally issued to the Erbprinz Regiment. The 1797 pattern is illustrated by Fig 21. Apart from the difference in field colour, all other detail was the same for both battalions: gold embroidery and cyphers (FF), beneath gold crowns with red linings, the central shield on a green mound with, behind the shield, white (hoist) and blue (fly) flags with gold finials, brown spontoons with white heads, gold leaves, ribbons and surround to the arms, gold crown lined red above the shield, and two supporters—a black bull with white horns and red tongue, and a golden griffin with red tongue. The arms were as follows:

1. The Duchy of Mecklenburg: black bull's head with red nose-ring and white horns on a yellow field.
2. Rostock: golden griffin with red tongue on blue field.
3. The principality of Schwerin: the arms of Rostock over a green field with a white border.
4. The principality of Ratzeburg: white cross and gold crown on a red field.
5. Stargard: white arm holding gold ring on a red field.
6. The principality of Wenden: black bull's head, white horns, red nose-ring, all on a yellow field.
7. The county of Schwerin (escutcheon overall): red over gold.

The arms were arranged in the following manner:

$$\begin{array}{ccc} 1 & & 2 \\ 3 & 7 & 4 \\ 5 & & 6 \end{array}$$

The flags were 90cm on the hoist and 110cm in the fly, and were carried on a stave with a gilt finial of pierced spearhead shape bearing the crowned monogram of the duke.

A Grenadier-Garde battalion was raised in 1810 and was presented with a white flag of similar design, except the arms were on a square rather than an oval shield, and the corner cyphers were surrounded by wreaths of palm and laurel leaves. The battalion defected to the Allies in 1813. The Line Infantry regiment was destroyed during the 1812 campaign.

21. Mecklenburg: obverse of the 1797 pattern issued to the 7th Rheinbund-Regiment in 1808 and carried until 1812.

21

In March of 1813 Mecklenburg joined the Allies against Napoleon. A regiment of Jäger zu Pferde was raised and presented with a white standard which bore on one side the inscription VON GOTT KOMMT MUTH UND STARKE in gold within a golden wreath of oak leaves, and on the other the arms of Mecklenburg within a similar wreath, all superimposed on a red cross.

Nassau

The principalities of Nassau-Usingen and Nassau-Weilburg joined the Rheinbund in 1806 and, along with Hohenzollern, Salm, Isenburg, Liechtenstein, Leyen and Aremberg, supplied 4,000 men, organized into a brigade of four battalions and a Jäger zu Pferde company. In 1809 the battalions were re-organized into the 2nd (1st Nassau) and 3rd (2nd Nassau) Rheinbund-Regiments, each of two battalions. The Jäger zu Pferde company was expanded to a regiment of two squadrons. These troops fought in the campaigns in Germany in 1806–07 and 1809, and in Spain 1808–13 (1st Nassau Regiment from 1810, and the 1st Squadron, Jäger zu Pferde in 1813 only).

On 16 November 1813 Nassau left the Rheinbund to join the Allies against Napoleon. The 2nd Infantry Regiment (Nassau-Weilburg) went over to the British on 10 December and was repatriated to Nassau with its flags, but the 1st Nassau Regiment (Nassau-Usingen) and Jäger zu Pferde Regiment were disarmed on 22 December and interned in Spain by the French.

For the 1814 campaigns Nassau raised a 3rd Infantry Regiment, a Landwehr Infantry Regiment, a Jäger corps, and 29 battalions of Landsturm. In 1815 Nassau contributed two infantry regiments, each of two Line and one Landwehr battalions.

During the 1806–13 period the two infantry regiments carried flags of the pattern illustrated in Plate D4: both sides were the same, with the lion of Nassau facing the hoist. The flags were 100cm on the hoist, 85 to 90cm in the fly, and were embroidered by the princesses of Nassau and the ladies of their court.

22. Nassau: reverse and obverse of the flag carried by the Landsturm Battalion Idstein Wehen in 1814.

Initially there was no distinction between the flags of the two regiments, or the battalions within each regiment, but after the battle of Medellin (1809) the 1st Battalion of the 2nd Regiment was granted the honour of carrying a likeness of the Médaille d'Or de la Bravoure on its flag, and after the combat at Mesas de Ibor two months later the same honour was granted to the regiment's 2nd Battalion. The flags of this regiment have survived, but do not bear portraits of any medals: possibly inscribed cravats were awarded, a more normal practice.

In 1814 the same flags appear to have been used by the 3rd Infantry Regiment. An example of the type of flag carried by the Landsturm battalions is illustrated in Fig 22, the flag carried by the Battalion Idstein Wehen: yellow field, green wreaths with red berries, the arms of Nassau under a gold crown lined red, all lettering black. The stave was painted blue and dark yellow in a spiral pattern and the finial was gilt. Other battalions carried similar flags, but with their own titles in the centre of the reverse.

The 1806–13 pattern flags were carried once again by the 2nd Regiment in the Waterloo campaign: it is not known if the other infantry regiment carried flags, and if so whether they were also of the old pattern.

No details are known of any standards which might have been carried by the Jäger zu Pferde Regiment.

Portugal

No precise details are known of the flags carried by the Portuguese Army prior to 1806, but a decree of 10 December 1801 mentions the existence of regulations for flags, and there are also records of flags being issued to infantry regiments in 1791 and 1792 at the scale of two per regiment. Those issued to the 2nd (Armada Real) Regiment in 1791 were made of crimson, white, dark blue, rose pink, gold and black silk, which suggests a similar pattern to that described below for the later period.

Another decree, of 19 May 1806, ordered the entire re-organization of the Army, creating new styles for the uniforms and new patterns (partly based on the earlier ones) for the regimental flags and standards. The decree included the following paragraphs on flags:

'(XXV) Each regiment of infantry and artillery to have two flags, one in the colours blue, white, scarlet and yellow, the other of the colour of the uniform lining appropriate to the regiment.

'(XXVI) Each regiment of cavalry to have four standards, distributed among the four squadrons in the following manner: the first squadron to have a white standard, the second red, the third yellow and the fourth blue.

'(XXVII) The flags will have a ribbon [i.e. cravat] of silk, in the colours of the collar and cuffs of the regiment, tied about the pole immediately below the pike head with the ends fringed. The standards will have, in the same style and the same place, a silken ribbon in the colour of the collar and cuffs of the respective units.

'(XXVIII) The flags and standards will have embroidered in the middle the Arms of the Realm, and below that the words "REGIMENTO Nº . . ." Those regiments to which the decree of 17 December 1795 granted the right to add the words "AO VALOR" to the name of the regiment [awarded to six regiments for their part in the operations against the French in 1793–95] will preserve the same distinction, having below the arms the legend "AO VALOR DO REGIMENTO Nº . . ."'

The 1795 inscriptions carried until 1806 were:

3rd Regiment: AO VALOR DO I REGIMENTO DE OLIVENÇA
4th Regiment: AO VALOR DO REGIMENTO DE FREIRE
6th Regiment: AO VALOR DO I REGIMENTO DE PORTO
13th Regiment: AO VALOR DO REGIMENTO DE PENICHE
18th Regiment: AO VALOR DO 2 REGIMENTO DE PORTO
19th Regiment: AO VALOR DO REGIMENTO DE CASCAES

The actual pattern of these flags and standards has been the subject of much speculation, for very little remains of the surviving examples: a single infantry flag of a volunteer regiment in the Museu Militar in Lisbon, but in extremely poor condition; no less than 18 different fragments in the Musée de

23. Portugal: battalion flag of the 9th Line Infantry, 1806 pattern. (The bugle horn is shown in error; this should be the ribbon and cross device shown correctly in Plate E1 and E2.)

24. Portugal: 1806 pattern for cavalry standards. See correction described under Fig 23.

1. 2nd Bn., 5th Rheinbund-Regt., 1812
2. 1st Bn., 5th Rheinbund-Regt., 1811
3. Denmark: Liveskadronen, Royal Horse Guards
4. Denmark: Jutland Light Dragoon Regt.

1

2

3

4

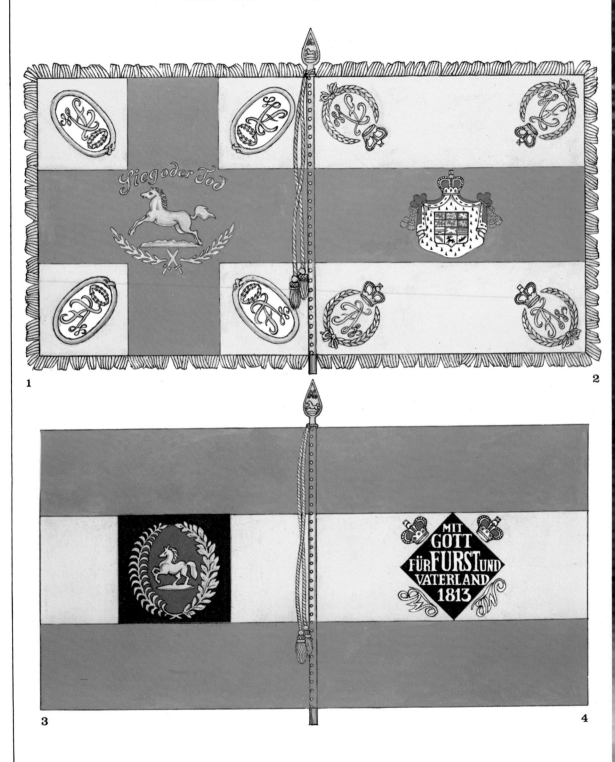

1

2

3

4

B

1 and 2.   Legion Hanovrienne, 1804–11
3.   Hesse-Kassel: Landwehr flag, 1814
4.   Hesse: Leibgarde zu Pferde, 1806–13

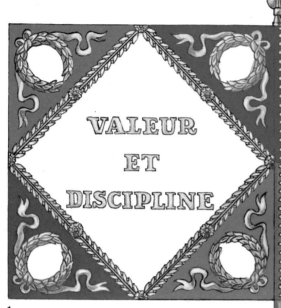

1

2

3

4

1 and 2   Netherlands: Line Infantry, 1806–10 pattern
3.   Netherlands: Militia unit, 1815
4.   Nassau: Line Infantry, 1806–13 pattern

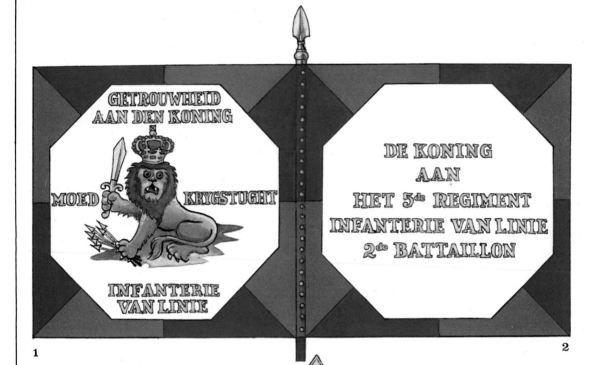

1

2

3

4

D

1. Portugal: Line Infantry 'King's Colour,' 1806 pattern
2. Portugal: Caçadores 'King's Colour,' 1813–14
3 and 4. Switzerland: 1798–1804 infantry pattern

1. Spain: Line Infantry Coronela, 1768 pattern
2. Spain: Line Infantry Ordenanza, 1768 pattern
3. Spain: Cavalry standard, 1768 pattern
4. Spain: Artillery standard, *c.*1715–1820

1

2

3

4

1. Sweden: Line Infantry Kompanifana, 1766 pattern
2. Sweden: Line Infantry Kompanifana, 1813–15
3. Sweden: Royal Swedois Regt., 1813–14
4. Sweden: Artillery standard, 1815

1

2

3

4

1 and 2.   Westphalia: Leibgarde zu Pferde, 1808–1812
3 and 4.   Westphalia: Leibgarde zu Pferde, 1812–13

l'Armée in Paris, but almost all so fragmented as to be incapable of yielding a reconstruction which can be guaranteed correct; a set of water colours by Sñr Palma Vaz of infantry and cavalry flags in the Portuguese Army Museum at Busaco; and in the same museum a display of many flags which were reconstructed for the occasion of the centenary of the Peninsular War in 1910.

There is one other source, a book entitled *Colleçcaon des novos uniformes da tropa portugueza*, Lisbon, 1806, which consists of 75 engraved and coloured plates depicting officers and men of the infantry and cavalry with the regulation uniforms of that date, and in the background of each plate there is visible the flag of the regiment to which the figure belongs. These flags are only lightly sketched but, together with the various decrees and regulations, and the fragments of items Aa 129, 131, 144, 145, 146 and 147–147^9 in the Musée de l'Armée catalogue, they do enable reconstructions of the Line Infantry flags and cavalry standards to be made—reconstructions which are in accordance with those produced by the Museu Militar in 1910.

The reconstructed 1806 pattern for the 'King's Colour' issued to infantry regiments is illustrated in Plate E1, which shows the obverse of the King's Colour of the 9th Line: the inscription round the edge of the central white field was not added until 1813–14 and then only on the flags of the 9th, 11th, 21st and 23rd Line: see below. It is assumed this flag would have been carried by the 1st Battalion.

The reconstruction of the 1806 pattern for the 'Regimental Colour' is illustrated in Fig 23, that of the 9th Line, presumably carried by the 2nd Battalion: yellow field, blue scroll with gold lettering, other detail as Plates E1 and E2.

The reconstruction of the basic 1806 pattern for cavalry standards is illustrated in Fig 24. (The bugle horn device below the central emblem in Figs 23 and 24 is an error, and should be a ribbon and cross as in the colour plates).

The reverse of these Colours and standards was of the same design as the obverse.

The inscriptions on the infantry flags (Section XXVIII above) were re-affirmed on 11 February 1807.

According to the decree of 19 May 1806, the army was divided into three grand divisions—North, Centre and South. All units belonging to the Northern Division were allocated uniform linings of yellow, those of the Centre Division white linings, and those of the Southern Division scarlet linings. Individual regiments within each division were identified by the colour of collar and cuffs. Therefore, the following listings define the cravat colour for all regiments, based on collar and cuff colours; and the fields of the Regimental Colours for infantry and artillery regiments, based on the coat lining colour.

Cavalry Regiments: field colour determined by squadron, not Division. Cravat colour: 1st–3rd Regiments, white; 4th–6th, scarlet; 7th–9th, yellow; 10th–12th, light blue.

Artillery Regiments: field colour scarlet for all four regiments. Cravat colour dark blue for all regiments. (This last does not agree with the dress regulations, which give red collar and cuffs for 1806–09.)

Infantry Regiments:

No	Name	Field	Cravat
1	Regt. de Lippe	white	dark blue & white
2	Regt. de Lagos	scarlet	dark blue & white
3	Regt. 1 de Olivença	yellow	dark blue & white
4	Regt. de Freire de Andrade	white	dark blue & scarlet
5	Regt. 1 de Elvas	scarlet	dark blue & scarlet
6	Regt. 1 de Porto	yellow	dark blue & scarlet
7	Regt. de Setubal	white	dark blue & yellow
8	Regt. de Castelo de Vide	scarlet	dark blue & yellow
9	Regt. de Viano	yellow	dark blue & yellow
10	Regt. de Lisboa	white	dark and light blue
11	Regt. de Penamacor	scarlet	dark and light blue
12	Regt. de Chaves	yellow	dark and light blue
13	Regt. de Peniche	white	white
14	Regt. de Tavira	scarlet	white
15	Regt. 2 de Olivença	yellow	white
16	Regt. de Vieira Teles	white	scarlet
17	Regt. 2 de Elvas	scarlet	scarlet
18	Regt. 2 do Porto	yellow	scarlet
19	Regt. de Cascais	white	yellow
20	Regt. de Campo Maior	scarlet	yellow
21	Regt. de Valença	yellow	yellow
22	Regt. de Serpa	white	light blue
23	Regt. de Almeida	scarlet	light blue
24	Regt. de Bragança	yellow	light blue

The 7th and 11th Caçadores (see below) had cravats of yellow and black.

25. Reuss: reverse of the flag carried by the Reuss Battalion from 13 February 1814.

A decree of 14 October 1808 created six battalions of caçadores, increased to 12 on 27 July 1811. These battalions, as light infantry, did not carry flags, but the 7th and 11th Battalions so distinguished themselves, especially at Vitória on 21 June 1813, that as a special honour these two battalions were granted flags. Part of the decree of

26. Spain: Coronela(?) of the Regiment de Infanteria de la Princesa.

13 November 1813, published as an Order of the Day of 13 March 1814 at the GHQ at Bordeaux, and referring to the bestowal of these flags, reads:

'And as the battalions of caçadores do not have flags they shall be granted to the two battalions Nº 7 and 11 mentioned above, to be carried on parades. . . . These flags are to be formed and divided [esquartelados—quartered] in the distinctive colours of my royal household, blue and scarlet, bearing my royal arms in the centre with, placed below, a palm encircled by the inscription *Distintos vos sereis na lusa historia/Com os louros que colhestes na Vitória.*'

(Roughly translated this means 'You will be distinguished in the history of Portugal by the laurels you won at Vitória'.)

As the caçadore flags were not granted until 1813–14, they do not appear in the 1806 uniform book and the only way they can be illustrated is by constructing an image from the verbal description quoted above. The Museu Militar found it impossible to construct the flags with any degree of certainty from that description alone, and it is doubtful if we shall ever know their exact form. We know how the fields of the Line regiments were divided into blue and red sections, and it is safe to assume that those of the 7th and 11th Caçadores would have followed the same pattern—though no mention is made of the yellow saltire. A reconstruction, following Ferreira Martin (in his history of the Portuguese Army) and Pereira de Sales, has been attempted here and is illustrated in Plate E2.

As the caçadores were organized as individual battalions, and this was a special award, it is most unlikely that a second flag would have been issued to the 7th and 11th Battalions.

The 9th, 11th, 21st and 23rd Line Regiments also distinguished themselves at Vitória and in the same decree (13/11/1813) were granted a special inscription to be added round the edge of the central white field bearing the royal arms. The inscription read: JULGAREIS QUAL HE MAIS EXCEL-LENTE? SE SER DO MUNDO REI OU DE TAL GENTE. (A rough translation is 'Judge which is better, to be king of the world or of such a people.) Plate E1 shows a flag bearing this inscription.

Of the flags carried by the various volunteer and militia units almost nothing is known. The single

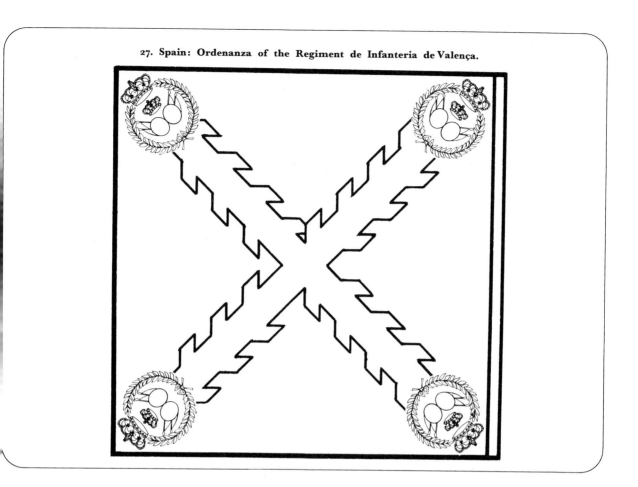

surviving Peninsular War flag in Lisbon belonged to the Voluntarios Reais do Comercio (Royal Merchant Volunteers), formed in 1808. This flag is in very poor condition, with many of the coloured panels of cloth no longer attached, but would appear to have conformed to the regulations of 19 May 1806. Of the flags held in Paris, some four or five of which were taken in April 1812 (possibly from Colonel Trant's rearguard at Mondego on the 14th—a force consisting entirely of militia units from the north), a few carry discernible variants to the regulations. N° 131, for example, has the large inverted bugle horn at the central coat of arms (see Figs 23 and 24) instead of the ribbon and cross: N° 145 is described as 'In the centre the arms of Portugal with a royal crown over an anchor'; and N° 147 as 'In the centre the arms of Portugal under a crown and surrounded by palm leaves of gold.'

The Loyal Lusitanian Legion was dressed, trained, equipped and operated as a Rifles unit:

it is most unlikely that it ever had any flags.

A Companhia de Guardas-Marinhas was formed by decree (14 December 1782) and an Admiralty order of 31 January 1801 refers to the flags of this company as an Estandarte and an Estandarte Real. Details are known of one of these standards, probably the royal one. It measures 108cm on the hoist and 110cm in the fly, and has a red field with gold fringe and gold cyphers in each corner within golden wreaths surmounted by gold crowns with red linings. In the centre of the obverse is a white oval bearing a portrait of the Virgin Mary in a blue cloak wrapped round a white gown, the oval being surrounded by an elaborate rococo design which includes a great wreath, all in gold, and surmounted by a gold crown lined red. The reverse bears in the centre the royal arms as for the infantry flags, with the same ribbon and cross below them, but in place of the trophy of arms there are two large anchors in gold which cross at the bottom edge of the central

27

29. Spain: Ordenanza of the Tercio Sagunto.

oval. Issuing from this cross point, and winding round the anchor's flukes to left and right is a white scroll edged gold and bearing in large gold letters the title COMP^a DE/GG MM.

This standard accompanied the detachment of marines which guarded the Portuguese Royal Family when it fled from Lisbon in November 1807. Consequently the standard survived the French occupation of Portugal and was returned to Portugal with the Royal Family in 1821.

Reuss

The only known flag for this German principality was one issued on 13 February 1814, by which time the Reuss contingent was part of the allied 6th German Corps. The flag was 123cm on the hoist and 110cm in the fly and was carried on a light brown stave about 300cm long with a finial in the form of the golden lion from the principality's arms. The flag had a yellow field, silver fringe, and bore on the reverse a red mantle lined ermine, with gold fringe, crown, cords and decoration. Arms: 1 and 4, black field, gold lion with red crown, claws and tongue; 2 and 3, white field, gold stork. (See Fig 25.) The obverse bore the motto WIR BAUEN AUF GOTT surrounded by a laurel wreath.

Spain

The flags carried by the regiments of the Spanish Army until at least 1808, when Napoleon put his brother Joseph on the throne, were of the designs laid down in the previous century. A decree of 22 October 1768 had ordered that every infantry regiment should have two flags, one per battalion, and each cavalry regiment one per squadron, with red 'ties', the latter meaning either cords or cravats, probably the former. It continued: 'The first one will be white with my royal coat of arms,

and the other white with the cross of Burgundy, and in both the coat of arms of the kingdoms or provinces should be included at the edge of each of the four corners, and the particular emblem they have had or have used with my royal approval.'

The cavalry standards in practice seem to have continued to follow the pattern laid down by an earlier decree (the royal coat of arms on the obverse, the arms of the regiment's province or kingdom on the reverse, both without the corner emblems) but on a white field instead of the 18th-century red field. One cavalry regiment did not use white for the fields of its standards—the Regiment Del Principe, which was awarded flags of purple (for the significance of this, see under Guards below) in commemoration of saving the Royal Walloon Guards at the battle of Zaragoza in 1710.

All these flags were rather small, the infantry ones being approximately 140cm square. The proportions of the various emblems varied from regiment to regiment because of the lack of a definitive drawn pattern. In general the royal arms occupied a large portion of the flag, not just the centre, while the cross of Burgundy tended to be wide rather than narrow, and the 'branches' were alternating on some flags, parallel on others. The emblems of the kingdoms and provinces also varied in size and richness of ornamentation, the latter probably dependent entirely upon the generosity of whoever paid for the flags.

The basic patterns for Line Infantry, as described by the 1768 decree, are illustrated in Plate F1 (the Coronela or King's Colour), and Plate F2 (the Ordenanza or Regimental Colour). The 1768 pattern for Line Cavalry is shown in Plate F3.

The foreign Line Infantry regiments (ten out of 45 in 1808) appear to have followed these regulations for their flags, with varying degrees of national distinction. For example, the three Irish regiments (Hibernia, Ultonia and Irlanda) each had a Coronela and Ordenanza as for the Spanish infantry regiments, with the single difference that the corner devices bore the Irish harp instead of the arms of a province or kingdom: see Plate F1. The flags of the Ultonia Regiment also had two additional distinctions: the quotation IN OMNES TERRAM EXHIBIT SONUS EORUM, added to comme-

morate the courage of the regiment at the battle of Campo Santo in Italy in 1743; and the battle honour BIDASSOA, granted in 1794 by Charles IV.

On the other hand, the flags of the Swiss infantry regiments do not appear to have conformed to the Spanish regulations, but had a distinctive Swiss appearance with Spanish emblems only sometimes added. Thus the Swiss regiment Bettschart in the Spanish service carried a much larger flag, 210cm on the hoist and 230cm in the fly, with a blue field bearing a white Maltese cross whose points reached to the four edges of the field, and with four white 'flames' issuing in a very narrow form from under the centre of the cross and broadening as they traversed the quarters of the field to each corner. In the canton, on the white flame and following the same angle as the flame, was a small portrait of the Madonna and Child, sitting on a throne, with behind one shoulder an angel, and behind the other God looking down from a cloud.

Other Swiss regiments carried similar flags but some had their fields divided into many wavy 'flames', with the cross of Burgundy overall. An unidentified flag of this type is preserved in the Salle Turenne (Paris catalogue Nª 160) and has a field divided into 24 flames of blue, white and yellow, with the red cross of Burgundy overall, but in addition carries a large emblem at the end of each arm of the cross in the Spanish fashion, identifying it as the Ordenanza. This emblem consists of crossed cannon and flags behind a shield with a crown above it, the shield bearing in the centre a large crescent with both points uppermost, above the crescent two small stars, and below it what appears to be part of a spontoon head or the top half of a fleur-de-lis (possibly the arms of the colonel?)

None of the regulations listed above make any mention of the flags to be carried by the troops of the Royal Household, but according to a manuscript in the Royal Palace in Madrid (*Teatro Militar del l'Europa*, by Marquis Alfonso Taccoli, and quoted in the *Enciclopedia Universal Illustrada*) they were as follows:

Guardia de Corps The Spanish Company had a red

POR EL REI FERNANDO VII

VENCER O MORIR

SV QVARTO VATA ᵒⁿ DER GVARDIAS

banner with silver embroidery, and bore in the centre the royal arms. Across the top of the arms was a white ribbon bearing the motto SOLVIT FORMIDINE TERRA. The Flemish Company had a yellow banner with silver embroidery, with in the centre a large oval showing the sea illuminated by a golden sun, the oval surrounded by a wide border containing the castles and golden lions of the royal arms. Across the top of this emblem was a white ribbon bearing the same motto as for the Spanish Company. The Italian Company had a banner of the same design as that of the Flemish Company, but on a green field.

Royal Spanish Guards The Coronela had a purple field, scattered with embroidered golden fleurs-de-lis. The Ordenanza flags were white, with the red cross of Burgundy bearing golden crowns at the end of each arm. In the centre were the royal arms with two golden lions as supporters.

Royal Walloon Guards The Coronela was as for the Ordenanza of the Royal Spanish Guards. The Ordenanza flags were of the same design but on a blue field.

Royal Italian Guards The Coronela was red with golden fleurs-de-lis embroidered upon it. The Ordenanza flags were white with the royal arms in the centre.

Royal Swiss Guards The Coronela was purple with golden fleurs-de-lis embroidered upon it. The Ordenanza flags were as for those of the Royal Italian Guards.

The purple used for the fields of the Royal regiments has its origins in medieval times. The correct colours for the arms of the royal houses of Aragon and Castile are red and yellow, and red, yellow and white respectively; but there is an ancient belief that the true colours of Castile were purple, yellow and white. Thus Ferdinand V, after the death of Isabella of Castile, formed the Halberdier Guards and ordered that one of their flags be in the purple colour of the House of Castile, with a medallion in the centre. When Philip IV (1621–65) created the Regiment of Foot Guards, their flags were again in the purple of the Royal House, the purple serving to show that these men belonged to a royal regiment, not a

32. Sweden: obverse of the 1766 pattern Liffana belonging to the Vastgota-Dals Infantry Regiment.

provincial or national one. This belief in purple as the true colour for Castile has continued even into the 20th century, and as late as 1968 it was put forward that the Spanish national flag should be in the colours red/yellow/purple instead of red/yellow/red.

The Royal Regiment of Artillery was created by the decree of 2 May 1710, article 21 of which stipulated that each battalion should have three flags, 'with some artillery emblem which will separate them from the infantry flags'. Nothing was said about the colour of the field, but as the Artillery was a royal regiment it is believed the fields were purple from the very beginning (see under Engineers below), while the regulations for Artillery in 1861 state that the banners and flags of the foot and horse artillery regiments would continue to be purple. An artillery flag carried during the Napoleonic Wars is illustrated in Plate F4.

Another royal decree, of 14 October 1803, created the first special troops of military engineers. It states: 'Each battalion will have a flag identical in size to the Infantry one; the first flag will be purple, with my royal coat of arms and the title REAL CUERPO DE ZAPADORES Y MINADORES [Royal Troop of Sappers and Miners]; the second once again purple, with the cross of Burgundy and the same title; on two of its corners it will have

lions, and on the other two it will have castles.'

Spain was 'occupied' by the French in 1807 (for the Franco-Spanish invasion of Portugal) and the Spanish Army at first co-operated with Napoleon, but when Joseph Bonaparte was made King of Spain in mid-1808 the whole of Spain united to throw out the French usurper. Those regiments of the former Regular Army which were still in Spain continued to use the flags described above, but the new units which were now formed, composed of volunteers, the former provincial and urban militias, and guerillas, all created individual flags of their own designs. It is impossible to generalise about these flags, but it is true to say that the majority of them bore some form of religious emblem, such as a crucifix, the Virgin Mary, saints, etc., while many others bore just a patriotic slogan such as FOR FERDINAND VII, or TO WIN OR DIE. Also, the more important the unit, the closer its flags tended to conform to the flag regulations of the old Regular Army.

The field colour of these flags also varied considerably, e.g. those of the Tercios de Migueletes de Cataluña were black with a Roman numeral to indicate their place amongst the tercios of that principality. However, the most common field colour was white. Several examples of such flags have been illustrated in the text:

Fig 26: obverse of the Coronela(?) of the Regiment de Infanteria de la Princesa, a Regular Army regiment initially raised in 1766. The design follows the official regulations quite closely, as one would expect in a former Regular Army regiment, but mixes the patterns for Coronela and Ordenanza in one flag: possibly the regiment had only the one flag, and this combination was deliberate.

Fig 27: obverse of the Ordenanza of the Regiment de Infanteria de Valença, another Regular Army regiment. The flag conforms to the 1728 decree in all respects, except the corner emblems are not enclosed in the standard pre-1808 framework: see the flags illustrated in Plate F. The corner wreaths shown here are green.

Fig 28: reverse of the Ordenanza of the 2nd Battalion, Regiment de Infanteria Imperial Alejandro. This regiment was raised in 1814. The flag conforms to the official regulations, except for the corner devices: the double-headed eagle bears the arms of Spain on the shield on its breast.

Fig 29: obverse of the Ordenanza of the Tercio Saguntino (Sagunto was called Murviedro at this date). This example follows the official regulations quite closely, but bears emblems of a religious nature. The field is white, the cross and Burgundy cross red, all lettering black. The Madonna is in pink, white (gown) and blue (cloak), with golden halo and green wreath. The flag is shown 'right way up' for clarity, but note it was actually flown 'sideways', with the small cross next to the stave.

Fig 30: obverse of the flag carried by the Volunteers of Ciudad-Rodrigo. The reverse bore a different design which included the name of the town. Colours unknown. This and Fig 27 are typical examples of the flags carried by newly raised units during the War of Independence.

Fig 31: obverse of the flag of the 4th Battalion, Royal Spanish Guards; white field, crimson lettering. (The reversed 'N' in Fernando appears thus on the original flag.) This battalion would have been quite justified in adopting a Coronela and Ordenanza of the statutory patterns, but chose instead a style typical of those flags carried by regiments raised after 1808.

After the War of Independence many flags of this nature were deposited in the Atocha Basilica in Madrid, and later moved to the Army Museum, where they have been preserved. On the other hand few of the Regular Army flags have survived, for many of those taken by the French were destroyed in Paris by an accidental fire in 1851, and most of the fragments now held there consist of the central royal coat of arms or the corner shields bearing the arms of provinces, cities or kingdoms.

King Joseph also formed a Spanish Army loyal to the French cause, consisting eventually of four Guard regiments and 14 Line: this was called the Army of King Joseph. A decree of 24 March 1809 stated that the infantry regiments of this army were to have flags of white taffeta, with a 'Bonapartic emblem' (possibly the Imperial golden eagle on a light blue shield) in the centre, and in each corner the number of the regiment in the centre of a star for Line regiments, and in the centre of a bugle horn for the two Light Infantry regiments. However, this decree was never put into effect, and so far as is known the Army of King Joseph did not receive flags.

33. Switzerland: flag of the 2nd Battalion of Line Infantry (from the canton of St Gallen) during the 1798–1803 period.

Sweden

Until 1809 the flags of the Swedish regiments in the dual kingdom of Sweden and Finland naturally followed the same patterns as those described earlier for Finland. During the 1792–1809 period, therefore, the Line Infantry regiments each had one Liffana for the first company, and one Kompanifana for each of the other companies in the regiment, of the 1766 pattern. The Liffana was white, the others in provincial colours. Both types were approximately 170cm on the hoist and 190cm in the fly, carried on white staves with gilt finials of spearhead-shape, pierced to show the sovereign's monogram. Cravats were in provincial colours.

The Liffana carried the Swedish royal arms in the centre, and in the canton a small coat of arms to indicate from which province the regiment came. The Kompanifana bore a provincial coat of arms in the centre. On all flags the obverse and reverse were of the same design.

The flags of the royal household regiments (Lifregementets) were all white, the Liffana having the royal arms in the centre, the Kompanifana a crowned royal monogram within palm leaves.

Fig 32 shows the basic design for infantry flags, the obverse of the Liffana carried by the Vastgota-Dals Infantry Regiment *circa* 1800: white field, black and yellow central insignia. This particular example survives in Stockholm and measures 151cm on the hoist, 174cm in the fly, and was carried on a stave 100cm long and with a diameter of 32mm. Another slightly different example of the 1766 pattern may be seen in Plate G1.

The cavalry had standards approximately 65cm square, the dragoons having swallow-tailed guidons 92cm on the hoist, 108cm in the fly overall. Both were white for the Lifstandar, in provincial colours for the Kompanistandaret. The Lifstandar had the royal arms in the centre and a provincial coat of arms in the canton, the Kompanistandaret a provincial coat of arms in the centre of the reverse, the royal cypher, crowned and flanked by palm leaves, on the obverse: see Figs 11 and 12 in the Finnish section. Both standards and guidons were fringed, and were carried on white staves for the Lifstandar, on staves painted in provincial colours for the Kompanistandaret. Cravats were in provincial colours.

In 1812 Marshal of France Jean-Baptiste Bernadotte, who had succeeded the weak Swedish king Charles XIII in 1809 as Crown Prince, allied Sweden with Britain, Prussia and Russia. Plate G2 illustrates a flag carried by the Varmlands Infantry Regiment during this period: other infantry regiments had flags of the same basic pattern. Plate G3 shows the unique flag carried by the Royal Swedois Regiment in 1813–14: this regiment was part of the Royal Swedish Army but was multi-national in character, a third of the men being French and many others German. The regiment may have participated in the Leipzig campaign: it certainly took part in the invasion of Norway in 1814. The regiment was disbanded in December 1814. Plate G4 shows the standard of the Vendes Artillery Regiment in 1815: at this date the Swedish artillery was organized in three regiments, each of two battalions.

The Kronprinsens Husarregemente of 1815 carried a small square standard of yellow cloth, bearing a small Swedish crown in each corner (tops pointing inwards) with, in the centre, a circular field bearing a sword, blade uppermost, over a Maltese cross turned through 45 degrees, with a small Swedish crown placed in the spaces between the arms of the cross, their bottom edges resting against the circular field. Above this device were crossed swords and a royal crown, and below it a sword, blade uppermost. No details are known of the standards of other cavalry regiments of this period.

Switzerland

The French 'liberated' the confederation of Swiss cantons in 1798 and established in its place the Helvetian Republic, which was to last until 1803. The Helvetian Republic was obliged to raise 18,000 men in six Demi-Brigades, each of three battalions, for the French service. These Demi-Brigades continued to serve the French until 1804, and an example of the type of flag carried by them until then is illustrated by Plate E3, a flag belonging to the 3rd Demi-Brigade.

On 27 September 1803 the six Demi-Brigades were ordered to re-organize as four Demi-Brigades, each of four battalions, and this was put into effect by 1805. On 12 August that year each of these new Demi-Brigades received an eagle with a flag of the 1804 French Line Infantry pattern on a provisional basis. The inscription on the white diamond of the obverse read L'EMPEREUR/DES FRANÇAIS/A LA ..me DEMI-BRIGADE/HELVÉTIQUE, and on the reverse VALEUR/ET DISCIPLINE. On 12 September each battalion was ordered to be issued with a flag of the 1804 pattern, inscribed on the obverse L'EMPEREUR/DES FRANÇAIS/AU ..me RÉGIMENT/SUISSE, and on the reverse VALEUR/ET DISCIPLINE/..me BATAILLON. These four Swiss regiments in the French service were never issued with the new flags of the 1812 pattern.

Fig 33 shows the design of one of the flags carried by the new republic's own regiments during the 1798–1803 period: green over red over yellow field, with all gold embroidery. The flag is 152cm on the hoist, 170cm in the fly, and was carried by a

34. Switzerland: flag carried by the men of Vaud in the period of the Helvetian Republic, 1798–1803.

LA PAIX

REPUBLIQUE HELVÉTIQUE

35. Switzerland: obverse of the flag carried by the Légion St Gallen in 1804.

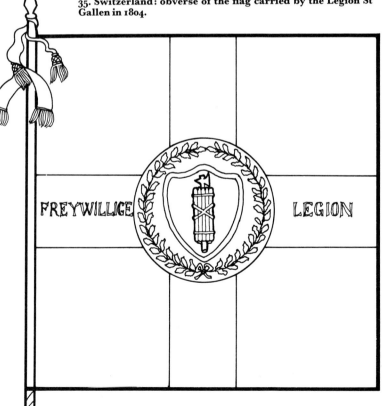

FREYWILLIGE

LEGION

battalion from the canton of St Gallen.

A flag carried by the men of Vaud during the same period is illustrated by Fig 34: green over red over yellow field, with all gold lettering. Size is 155cm on the hoist, 165cm in the fly. The Helvetian Regiment of Jäger zu Pferde carried during the 1798–1803 period a standard divided horizontally into three sections, green over red over yellow, with a fringe of the same three colours intermingled. Size was 90cm on the hoist, 72cm in the fly, and the flag was carried on a stave painted with a spiral pattern in the national colours. This regiment was raised in the canton of Zürich.

In 1803 Napoleon re-established the ancient confederation of 13 cantons, but added six others: it was from this date that the name of Switzerland was first officially given to the confederation of Swiss cantons. The troops of the cantons carried a variety of flags as before, and an example is illustrated by Fig 35, that of the Légion St Gallen in 1804: green field, white cross, green central circle bearing in gold the arms of St Gallen, and to

either side gold lettering. The flag is 183cm square and was carried on a stave painted in a green and white spiral pattern.

The militia of Tessin carried in 1809 a square flag with an overall white cross, as for St Gallen, but 1 and 3 were red, 2 and 4 blue. The Vaud militia also had a square flag, divided in half horizontally, the top half white and bearing in script the slogan LIBERTÉ ET PATRIE, the bottom half green and bearing the single word VAUD. This flag was carried from 1803 to 1842. The infantry of Bern had from 1804 a square red flag, with the overall white cross, and in each quarter two wavy black 'flames'. The Neuenburg militia carried a similar flag, but all white with red flames, from 1806 to 1815. In 1814 the artillery corps of Geneva carried the flag illustrated by Fig 36: white field bearing the arms of Geneva (black eagle with red crown, beak and claw on yellow, and yellow key on red) over a trophy of arms, with a lion and two laurel sprigs below, all in their proper colours and on a green mound. Above the arms is a golden sun burst, and above that a blue scroll. Lettering and date are gold, as is the fringe. Size is 62cm on the hoist, 75cm in the fly.

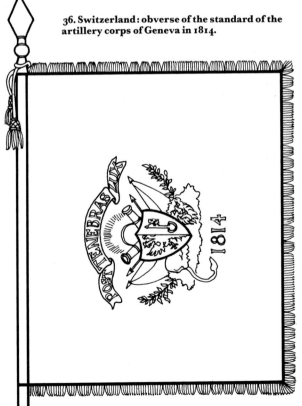

36. Switzerland: obverse of the standard of the artillery corps of Geneva in 1814.

Westphalia

The kingdom of Westphalia was formed by Imperial decree on 15 November 1807 and given to Jerome, favourite brother of Napoleon. Initially containing the lands of Hesse-Kassel and Brunswick, the kingdom was greatly increased in size in 1810 by the addition of Hanover. In 1812 the northern part of the kingdom, approximately a third of the total area, was incorporated into France. The kingdom disintegrated in September 1813 following the loss of some 27,000 men in Russia and further defeats, and defection by some regiments, during the 1813 campaigns.

The Line Infantry regiments received their first flags in the summer of 1808, at the scale of one per battalion. The flags followed closely the French 1804 pattern, with a dark blue field, white central diamond, and all gold embroidery. They were approximately 85–90cm square. In the canton corner and bottom fly corner were golden eagles within a laurel wreath, and in the other two corners the king's 'JN' monogram. The central diamond on the obverse bore the inscription LE ROI/DE WESTPHALIE/AU .. RÉGIMENT/D'INFANTERIE/DE LIGNE, and on the reverse VALEUR/ET DISCIPLINE/..me BATAILLON. The flags were carried on blue staves, 170cm long, with a plain spearhead-shaped finial.

The two battalions of Guard Infantry (Grenadiers and Jägers) received flags of a similar pattern on 1 July 1808 but, of course, with different inscriptions: on the obverse LE ROI/DE WESTPHALIE/AU BATAILLON DE/GRENADIERS GARDES, and on the reverse VALEUR/ET DISCIPLINE. All four corner wreaths were left empty on both sides. The spearhead-shaped finial was gilt and bore the monogram of the king. The stave was white.

In 1810 new flags were issued to the Line Infantry. These were of the same size and design as before, but with the inscriptions now in German and with slightly different corner emblems. The pattern is illustrated by Fig 37: dark blue field, white central diamond, all other detail gold. A third battalion of Guard, the Jäger-Carabinier d'Elite, received a flag of this pattern on 19 May 1811, with the necessary difference to the inscription on the obverse.

In 1812 another regiment was added to the Guard infantry, the Régiment de Fusiliers de la Reine (two battalions) and these battalions received flags of a new design on 22 November. The other infantry battalions of the Guard also received new flags in 1812, and all these flags were of the new pattern; a dark blue field bearing a broad white saltire. Plate H3 and H4 show the basic design of obverse and reverse, though the inscription on the obverse varied: the grenadiers' flag, for example, bore DER KÖNIG/VON WESTPHALIEN/DEM BATAILLON/GRENADIER-GARDE. The stave was now painted in blue and white spirals.

The cavalry regiments were issued with standards, 60cm square, in 1808. These were dark blue with a broad white saltire, and bore round the sides of the obverse the eagle of Westphalia in gold, and on the reverse the royal arms of the kingdom in the centre and the royal cypher round the sides. See Plate H3 and H4 for the basic design: the

regimental inscriptions on the centre of the obverse were in French.

The squadron of Garde du Corps and the squadron of Chevau-légers de la Garde each received a 60cm square standard on 1 July 1808. These were of the French 1804 pattern, as illustrated by Plate H1 and H2. Initially the inscriptions were in French, but these standards were soon replaced by others with the inscription in German, as illustrated.

The Line cavalry received new standards in 1812, again of the 1808 pattern but with the inscriptions now in German. Fig 38 shows the standard of the 1st Hussars at this date: dark blue field, white saltire, all gold embroidery except the royal arms in their proper colours. New standards were issued in 1813 after the débâcle of 1812: these were divided vertically into two halves, that nearest the hoist being dark blue, the other white. Inscriptions across these flags were in gold and in German gothic script.

The Guard Cavalry received a new pattern on 1 March 1812, again 60cm square, and of the design illustrated by Plate H3 and H4. Only that of the Leibgarde zu Pferde has survived, but the standard of the Chevau-légers de la Garde squadron should have been identical.

The Plates

A1: 2nd Battalion, 5th Rheinbund-Regiment, 1812 (reverse)
Presented to the Lippe battalion in 1812; see text under 'Anhalt' for description of obverse. The arms illustrated are: 1 Schwalenberg, 2 Ameide, 3 Saxony, 4 Zerbst.

A2: 1st Battalion, 5th Rheinbund-Regiment, 1811 (obverse)
Issued to replace that lost at La Bisbal in September 1810; the reverse was identical.

A3: Denmark: Liveskadronen, Royal Horse Guards (reverse)
This unit of some 200 men guarded the sovereign

and patrolled the coasts near Copenhagen; they saw action in 1807 in defence of that city.

A4: Denmark: Jutland Light Dragoon Regiment (obverse)
This pattern was used by all light dragoon regiments, the field being in the regimental facing colour.

B1, B2: Brunswick: Herzogsfahne, 1st Line Battalion, 1815
The reverse and obverse of the flag carried at the time of the Waterloo campaign.

B3, B4: Brunswick: Herzogsfahne, 2nd Line Battalion, 1815
Reverse and obverse respectively. The Bataillonsfahne of the 1st Line Bn. is illustrated as Fig 4, and that of this battalion as Fig 5.

C1, C2: Hanover: Légion Hanovrienne infantry battalions, 1804–05
Reverse and obverse of the flag carried by the Hanoverian infantry in French service. The Colours of the King's German Legion, the Hanoverians in British service, are illustrated and described in *Flags of the Napoleonic Wars (2)*, Men-at-Arms 78.

C3: Hesse-Kassel: Landwehr infantry battalion, 1814
Flag carried by one of nine battalions raised to fight against the French.

C4: Hesse: Leibgarde zu Pferde, 1806–13 (obverse)
This 1770 standard measured 56 by 54cm.

D1, D2: Netherlands: Line Infantry, 1806–10 pattern
Flag of the Kingdom of Holland, basically of French 1804 pattern.

D3: Netherlands: Militia unit, 1815
It is believed that Line and Jäger regiments carried flags of a similar design but in different colours.

D4: Nassau Line Infantry, 1806–13 pattern (obverse)
The reverse was identical, with the lion of Nassau facing the hoist.

37. Westphalia: reverse and obverse of the 1810 Line Infantry pattern.

E1: Portugal: 'King's Colour', 9th Line Infantry, 1806 pattern

The inscription round the central white field was not added until 1813–14.

E2: Portugal: 'King's Colour', 7th Caçadores, 1813–14

Special colour awarded for valour to the 7th and 11th Caçadores but not carried in battle.

E3, E4: Switzerland: Infantry Demi-Brigade, 1798–1804

Reverse and obverse of a flag carried by the 3rd Demi-Brigade Helvétique from 1798 to 1804; it was 163cm square. The central emblems were the same for all six Swiss Demi-Brigades, but the pattern of the field was different for each unit.

F1: Spain: Coronela, Irlanda Infantry Regiment (obverse)

The reverse was of the same design. Other Line Infantry regiments used the same pattern but with the arms of their province or kingdom in the corner emblems.

F2: Spain: Ordenanza, Macarquibir Infantry Regiment (obverse)

The reverse was identical. Other Line Infantry regiments used the same design but, again, with different province or kingdom arms in the corner emblems.

F3: Spain: Cavalry standard, 1768 pattern (obverse)

According to the 1768 decree the standards were to be identical to the Line Infantry flags, but in fact they were not. Firstly, the standards were fringed; secondly, they bore no corner emblems; and thirdly, regimental distinction was achieved by the devices carried in the centre of the reverse.

F4: Spain: Artillery standard, c.1715–1820

In royal purple, this flag was carried during the 18th century and apparently up to the end of the Napoleonic period.

G1: Sweden: Kompanifana, Vastgota Infantry Regiment, c.1766–1809 (reverse)

The field is in the colours of the province and the shield bears the provincial arms. The obverse bore the same design.

38. **Westphalia: obverse of the standard carried by the 1st Hussars in 1812.**

G2: Sweden: Kompanifana, Varmlands Infantry Regiment, 1815 (obverse)

The pattern carried in the period 1813–15, after Bernadotte allied the country with Britain, Prussia and Russia. The reverse bore the same design.

G3: Sweden: Royal Swedois Regiment, 1813–14

As far as is known both sides of the flag carried by this foreign unit were identical.

G4: Sweden: Hedersstandar, Vendes Artillery Regiment, 1815 (obverse)

At this date Sweden had three artillery regiments each of two battalions.

H1, H2: Westphalia: Leibgarde zu Pferde, 1808–12

Reverse and obverse of the cavalry standard carried by this household unit from 1 July 1808 to 1 March 1812.

H3, H4: Westphalia: Leibgarde zu Pferde, 1812–13

Reverse and obverse of the pattern which replaced the above from March 1812.

Notes sur les planches en couleur

A1 Présenté au bataillon Lippe en 1812, ce drapeau porte les armoiries de Schwalenberg, Ameide, Saxonie, Zerbst. **A2** Les deux faces de ce drapeau sont semblables; il fut présenté pour remplacer celui qui fut perdu à La Bisbal en septembre 1810. **A3** Indépendament de la garde de la Maison du Roi, ce régiment vit le feu pendant la défense de Copenhague en 1807. **A4** Le même dessin fût utilisé par tous les régiments de dragons légers, mais la couleur dépendait des parements régimentaux.

B1, B2 L'avers et le revers du drapeau porté pendant la campagne de Waterloo. **B3, B4** Avers et revers du drapeau de temps de Waterloo. Chaque bataillon portait également un 'Bataillonsfahne': celui du premier bataillon est montré ailleurs en figure 4, celui du deuxième bataillon en figure 5.

C1, C2 Avers et revers du drapeau porté par l'infanterie hanovrienne au service de la France. Les drapeaux hanovriens au service britannique—'la légion allemande du Roi'—sont montrés dans Men-at-Arms 78, 'Flags of the Napoleonic Wars (2)'. **C3** Drapeau de l'un des neufs bataillons levé pour combattre les français. **C4** Ce drapeau est d'un modèle datant de 1770.

D1, D2 Les drapeaux du Royaume de Hollande étaient essentiellement de modèle français, M1804. **D3** On pense que l'infanterie de Ligne et les régiments Jäger portaient des drapeaux de dessins similaires, mais à couleurs différentes. **D4** Le revers était identique, avec le lion face au poteau.

E1 L'inscription fut ajoutée en 1813–14, pour signaler le courage du régiment. **E2** Les bataillons Caçadore ne portaient normalement pas de drapeaux, mais celui-ci lui fût présenté en 1813–14 pour signaler le courage du régiment pendant la bataille de Vitoria. **E3, E4** Avers et revers du drapeau de la 3ème Demi-brigade Helvétique: les six demi-brigades avaient le même emblème central, mais le dessin du reste du drapeau était différent pour chaque unité.

F1, F2 Le revers était identique. Tous les régiments avaient le même dessin, sauf les armoiries des provinces des emblèmes dans le coin. **F3** Le décret de 1768 stipulait que les étendards de la cavalerie devaient être les mêmes que ceux de l'infanterie, mais ils étaient en fait différents. Ils avaient des franges, ils n'avaient pas d'emblèmes dans le coin, et l'emblème du centre variait selon l'unité. **F4** Ce drapeau de poupre royale semble avoir été porté du début du 18ème siècle jusqu'à la fin des guerres napoléoniennes.

G1 L'avers était identique—fond aux couleurs de la province, avec les armoiries de la province sur le blason. **G2** Le revers de ce drapeau, porté pendant la période suivant l'alliance de la Suède de Bernadotte avec l'Angleterre, la Prusse et la Russie, était le même que sur cette illustration. **G3** Autant que l'on sache, les deux faces du drapeau de ce régiment étranger étaient identiques.

H1, H2 Avers et revers de l'étendard porté par cette unité de gardes de 1808 à 1812. **H3, H4** Avers et revers du dessin qui remplaça celui du haut à partir de Mars 1812.

Farbtafeln

A1 Diese Fahne, dem Lippe Bataillon im Jahre 1812 überreicht, trägt das Wappen von Schwalenberg, Ameide, Sachsen, Zerbst. **A2** Beide Seiten dieser Fahne waren gleich: sie wurde überreicht, um die bei La Bisbal im September 1810 verlorene zu ersetzen. **A3** Ausser der Bewachung des königlichen Haushalts, kämpfte dieses Regiment bei der Verteidigung Kopenhagens im Jahre 1807. **A4** Dasselbe Muster wurde von allen Leichten Dragoner Regimentern benutzt, jedoch die Farbe wechselte mit der Besatzfarbe der Regimentsuniform.

B1, B2 Rück- und Vorderseite der in der Schlacht bei Waterloo getragenen Fahne. **B3, B4** Rück- und Vorderseite der Fahne zum Zeitpunkt von Waterloo. Jedes Bataillon trug auch eine Bataillonsfahne: die der 1. Bataillons ist woanders als Fig. 4, und die des 2. Bn. ist in Fig. 5 gezeigt.

C1, C2 Rück- und Vorderseite der von der hanoverischen Infanterie im französischen Dienst getragenen Fahne. Die Fahnen der Hanoveraner im britischen Dienst—'des Königs Deutsche Legion'—sind gezeigt in Men-at-Arms 78, *Flags of the Napoleonic Wars (2)*. **C3** Die Fahne einer der neun Bataillone, aufgestellt um gegen die Franzosen zu kämpfen. **C4** Diese Fahne ist die des Musters von 1770.

D1, D2 Die Fahnen des Königreiches Holland waren im Grunde von Französischem Muster nach dem Entwurf von 1804. **D3** Man glaubt, dass Linien-Infanterie und Jägerregimenter Fahnen von ähnlichem Entwurf trugen, jedoch in unterschiedlichen Farben.

E1 Die Inschrift wurde erst im Jahre 1813–14 hinzugefügt, um die Tapferkeit des Regiments kundzutun. **E2** Die Caçadore Bataillone trugen normalerweise keine Fahnen, jedoch diese wurde im Jahre 1813–14 präsentiert, um die Tapferkeit des Regiments bei der Schlacht von Vitoria anzuerkennen. **E3, E4** Rück- und Vorderseite der Fahne der 3. Demi-brigade Helvétique; alle sechs demi-brigades hatten die gleichen Embleme in der Mitte, jedoch das Muster der übrigen Fahne unterschied sich für jede Einheit.

E1, E2 Die Rückseite war dieselbe. Alle Regimenter hatten denselben Entwurf, ausser den provinziellen Wappen in den Eckemblemen. **E3** Die Verordnung von 1768 bestimmte, dass die Standarten der Kavallerie dieselben sein sollten, als die Fahnen der Infanterie, aber sie unterschieden sich in Wirklichkeit. Sie waren mit Fransen besetzt; sie hatten keine Eckembleme; und das Emblem in der Mitte unterschied sich von Einheit zu Einheit. **F4** Diese Fahne von königlichem purpur scheint vom frühen 18. Jahrhundert bis nach der napoleonischen Periode getragen worden zu sein.

G1 Die Vorderseite war dieselbe—ein Feld in der Farbe der Provinz, mit dem provinziellen Wappen auf dem Schild. **G2** Die Rückseite dieser Fahne, getragen in der Periode nachdem Bernadotte Schweden mit Britannien, Preussen und Russland alliierte, war dieselbe wie hier abgebildet. **G3** Soweit wie bekannt, waren beide Seiten der Fahne dieses fremden Regiments gleich. **G4** Zu dieser Zeit hatte Schweden drei Artillerieregimenter, jedes bestehend aus zwei Bataillonen.

H1, H2 Rück- und Vorderseite der Standarte, von dieser Garde-einheit von 1808–12 getragen. **H3, H4** Rück- und Vorderseite des Musters, das das obere vom März 1812 an ersetzte.